Tending Angels
Stories From the Frontlines of Heaven and Earth

Tending Angels
Stories From the Frontlines of Heaven and Earth

Sherry Cothran

Edited by Tisha Martin

Copyright © 2017 by Sherry Cothran

All rights reserved. This book or any portion thereof may not be reproduced or used in any manner whatsoever without the express written permission of the publisher except for the use of brief quotations in a book review or scholarly journal.

First Printing: 2017

New World Vultures Publishing
Chattanooga, TN 37411

www.sherrycothran.com

U.S. trade bookstores and wholesalers: Please contact Tel: 629-888-3603 or email info@sherrycothran.com

For Herman and Mary

Contents

Acknowledgements..ix
Preface..vii

Introduction..1

The Church and the Angels

  1: Have You Been Living Under a Rock?......................6
  2: The Holy, Homeless Family..9
  3: Corona and the Broken Church................................15
  4: The Rock of a Thousand Flaming Arrows...............21
  5: It's Time to Call the Experts....................................29
  6: You Can't Play a Player..33
  7: It's Hard to Know Exactly What to Do..................37
  8: Where Your Joy Meets the World's Pain...............46

Homilies & Meditations

  9: A Frosty, White Morning...51
  10: Huldah and the End of the World.........................54
  11: A Girl Doesn't Dream of Becoming a Prostitute...58
  12: Learning to Slay the Dragons Within...................61
  13: The Gift of the Ashes..65
  14: The Alleluia Pulpit: Singing with Emmy Lou.......68
  15: Peace Be Still: Giving Thanks as a Rebellious Act...72
  16: The Finding Your Voice Pose................................76
  17. Woman Gone Fishing, Be Back…Maybe............81
  18: Growing Hollow..87

Acknowledgements

To those who shared their stories with me. May your witness rise up to inspire us all to love and heal one another. To my husband, Patrick, I'm deeply grateful for your love and care in my life. Thanks to my spiritual mentor, Grady Wade, who taught me to see beauty in the impossible and so much more. Thanks to the church communities who inspired these stories. Gratitude to my editor, Tisha Martin and my literary agent, Rachelle Gardner. Thanks to friends and family for your inspiration, support and encouragement.

Preface

This book is a collection of stories, meditative essays and homilies originally shared, in shorter form, on my first blog, "Peddling Hope in Dystopia." Inspired by people who were often rejected because they bore the label of refugee, homeless, immigrant and poor; who came together in a haven inhabited by God in human skin. I landed there while attending seminary at Vanderbilt Divinity, in the process of becoming an ordained minister in the United Methodist church. I intended to be there a year and I ended up staying almost a decade as the senior pastor.

I was engaged in an effort to revitalize a crestfallen, urban church and fill it with people. However, instead of packing the pews with upwardly mobile professionals, though we did bring in a few of those, we filled our fellowship hall with the homeless; our extra rooms with programs for refugees; our basement with a food pantry to fight hunger and our extra chapel with programs for immigrants. The stories, essays and homilies in this book were inspired by my experiences in this place.

My encounters led me to see the sacred face of homelessness, and to think often of that phrase from Hebrews 13:2, that in showing hospitality to strangers I just might be "tending angels, unaware." The irony is that as I was trying to help others, I was the one who was changed.

I had followed my intuition to this place, a unique church I came to call the "frontlines of heaven and earth."

A few years before, I had left a career as the lead singer of a popular rock band. In the shadow of Nashville's Music City skyline, a city that had once held for me a hit song on rock radio, several faithful fans, a songwriting and record deal on a major label; I presided over funerals, delivered sermons, served communion to the faithful few and cooked meals for the homeless. I was in the same city, but in many ways, I was on the other side of the world. These essays represent some of the wisdom I gleaned from this place and express the ways my soul began to come to life through service to others.

The names have been changed in these stories to respect and protect the identities of the people.

I hope the book inspires others to get involved with programs that address change at the root level of human suffering in our nation. Systemic poverty, homelessness, and hunger can all be traced to the lack of human connection. Deep, unhealed wounds in all of us can often find a source of healing as we decide to reach out to one another in love and kindness, and develop networks of trust and community. As we find the common ground of trust, we can begin to heal and help one another.

It is my hope that these stories and the work I've done with music and video (See "Tending Angels Music Video," YouTube) will show the sacred face of homelessness and inspire others to loving action.

Introduction

Every Thursday, a room full of hungry, exhausted people who had no place to call home would gather at the urban church where I have served as pastor for the past decade. For many of them, the free, community dinner would be their one square meal for the week. Quite often, due to the irritation of hunger, tensions arose, sometimes with the threat of violence.

One evening, an impatient attendee pulled out a gun, brandishing it in the air, threatening to shoot if he wasn't first in line. Ten minutes later, the police arrived and, placing the inebriated man in handcuffs, discovered that the gun was actually an impressive fake.

A toy.

What makes this story and this place unique is that as we watched the police release him from his handcuffs, we prepared a takeout box full of dinner and set it aside for him. He came meekly to the side door with an apology, we handed him a hot meal and sent him away with a warning and a blessing.

After the incident, Jay, one of our regulars, a man who suffered from homelessness, noticed that I was a little shaken up. He pulled me aside, touched me gently on the elbow, leaned in close and said assuredly, "We'll never let anyone harm you; we're keeping watch over you."

This type of encounter would repeat more than a few times, thankfully, only once with a perceived weapon, (not counting the kitchen knife that ended up in the hands of one of our regulars who suffered from mental illness.) Tense moments between strangers turned into opportunities for the sacred to move among rejected and traumatized people with empty bellies and wounded spirits. I came to call it the "frontlines of heaven and earth." Where abandoned people came to feel love, warmth and be treated as human beings. Where these same people, through exchanges of kindness, often left me with the distinct feeling that I might be, as the Apostle Paul said, "tending angels, unaware."

As senior pastor, serving the kind of church Pope Francis has called "a triage hospital on the frontlines of the world's pain," working among people who bore the labels of immigrant, refugee, homeless, and poor; I have come to find that these are the kinds of places where the face of Christ-- the great Wounded Healer—can still be seen.

Here, I came to experience the wonder of the irony that as I tried to bind up the wounds of the brokenhearted, I was the one who was healed. As the poet Rumi said, "The wound is the place where the light enters you."[i]

As my heart was broken in these encounters, a wonderful thing happened. I suddenly began to have access to a deeper and stronger love hidden inside of me. It led me to understand that we all have love inside of us, waiting to be expressed. Sometimes we have to risk opening our hearts to people who are different, to the rejected ones of our communities and world, feeling their sorrow, hearing their stories, being moved by their pain, so this love can rise up out of us. We need encounters like these so that we can see it and believe it's actually there: God's love, at the core of us all. Sometimes our hearts must break to know what really holds us together.

As Jean Vanier said, "We are healed by those we reject."[ii] These encounters of loving and embracing some of the most rejected people in our world became moments of heartbreak and healing together.

"Tending Angels" is a collection of essays in two parts. The first section are stories that initially took form on my first blog, "Peddling Hope in Dystopia." I began the blog to share what I was seeing as I was shocked by the amount of homeless children, families, elderly and veterans in our community as well as teenagers. From my vantage point as a pastor, I could see in plain sight the people in our society that remain largely hidden. I felt that if I could share this unique perspective of their stories, it might open a new window and inspire people to take the risk of reaching out. These essays have been expanded for this collection.

The second section includes meditative essays from my own spiritual journey as well as homilies based on some Bible stories involving women that have been particularly formative for me. These appeared in various versions on my former blog as well and have also been expanded for this collection.

All together, these are the stories of how a haven for some of the most rejected people in the world became a place inhabited by God in human skin, in which it seemed the angels were pointing the way. These are a few of the experiences that unfolded while I was "tending angels, unaware."

The Church and the Angels

1. Have You Been Living Under a Rock?

I recently heard someone say this in a riveting speech about the many faces of Jesus: "I am careful when I go around corners for I never know when I might meet Messiah."

Today, a man in his mid to late fifties walked around the corner and into the door of the church, along with the shuffle of the homeless making their way into the weekly meal. He asked to see the pastor.

I said, "I'm the pastor."

He looked at me for a moment and said meekly, "I've never seen a female pastor before."

I was in a chompy mood. "Have you been living under a rock?"

To which he earnestly replied, "Yes. Yes, I am here from Iraq!"

I said a bit more slowly and deliberately, "No, I asked you if you had been living under a rock."

His face was blank.

If I had suffered from the desensitizing that comes with job, he certainly brought me back to my senses.

"Did you know they just killed fifty-two Christians in Iraq?" he exclaimed. "My church was bombed. We had to get out. You've heard of the war, right?" He kept reminding me that he had been a professor in Baghdad, teaching civil engineering and had maintained a comfortable life for his family. It was his mantra.

I asked him to sit down and tell me his story. He picked up a piece of paper and ghost wrote the terms of the "criminal government"—that's what he called them.

He said, "They give you three options: (1) give them one of your daughters, (2) pay them off, or (3) vacate your home and let them have it. The alternative is death. We got out by way of a connection with the U.S. Army which led to a connection which led to a connection. Two weeks later, we were on a plane, all of our belongings sold for cheap. Flying out of hell."

I think I began tearing up when he said, "They force you to give away your daughters." We know what happens to the daughters, it's a terror I cannot fathom.

Today, he was the Messiah who greeted me around the corner, fresh from the bloody cross, asking me to touch his scars. I'm so glad I did.

The scars carry in them all the daughters and the persecuted and the bombed-out countries that once resembled home. I understand that his scars are also mine. We are connected, and here is my brother in shock, in pain, in disbelief.

I have a role to play in his healing. I keep a church going that keeps a community of agencies going by offering space, support and radical hospitality. Within these agencies, specialized people reach out to communities of refugees, hungry, poor, imprisoned, homeless, sick, and needy. I can't do all of these things, but I can play my part as pastor, although some days I may be a bit bedraggled, chompy, and insensitive, I am at least wise enough to know when it's time sit at the feet of a stranger, who may also be my teacher, and listen.

As Christians, we have a role to play on behalf of the disposable daughters and the dispossessed world. That role has to do with reclaiming unity and realizing we are connected to those we may consider enemy through the command to love them. Our only real hope lies in our ability to embrace love at any cost.

"I am careful when I go around corners, for I never know when I may meet Messiah."

2. The Holy, Homeless Family

Occasionally I meet a holy family. This is my term for a homeless family with a baby. I call them holy because I always think of the traveling Mary and Joseph, rejected and forced outside, exposed to the elements, with the task of doing something Divine, giving birth to the Messiah.

Such a family walked into the community meal with a baby boy, not quite a year old, with blue eyes and blonde, curly ringlets. The couple had become newly homeless and were living in their car. I tried many different techniques to help them get into housing, working with other agencies, helping them with paper work, but nothing stuck. Even with all my best efforts, it seemed I was unable to find a solution for this family. The layers of their predicament were thick and seemingly impenetrable. They would appear and disappear with great irregularity.

Randomly, they would come into the meal, covered in grease, dirt, and the fatigue of the streets. I would hold the baby, give them supplies, sometimes put them up in a hotel—and my heart would break again. The church did as much as we could financially to help them but after a year of coming and going, they just couldn't get on their feet. It was so discouraging.

One Thursday night, one of my new mothers from the church came to the meal and noticed that the baby, now almost two years old, had blackened feet. She took a wash cloth and some soap from the kitchen and washed his feet. I had bought two gallons of milk for the meal that night, and she filled a bottle with fresh milk and fed him. The baby laughed at her, feeling safe in her arms. She noticed the dark circles under his eyes, and how tired the baby seemed.

She called me that night after the meal, crying.

"I don't know what to do, I can't stop thinking about this baby," she said through tears. "He just looked at me with his eyes, it was like he was crying for help and I just feel like I have to do something."

I tried to console her. I knew she had made a connection with the baby boy and that he reminded her so much of her own little boy. Her heart was genuinely breaking over the situation.

I assured her I would check further into what some of the options might be, though there didn't seem to be any great ones presenting themselves immediately.

There was the Department of Children's Services that we could call to come and investigate options for the baby's safety. I explained to her that I'd done everything in my power to try and get them to commit themselves to the family shelter, but they would have to split up and they refused to do so.

She wouldn't let it go, her heart had become involved. "I have some money if you think it would help, I can get together some supplies for them, whatever you think."

"I'll look into it this week," I said, and thanked her for her generous offer.

The next day I made some phone calls, tried to track down the couple, but they were nowhere to be found. They had no address other than their car, no one seemed to know them, they were part of a hidden population and they were hidden well.

After church on Sunday the young mother lingered, sitting in the back of the church crying.

Now there are few women in my church from Africa, they are refugees of war-torn countries like Sierra Leone and Sudan. They knew something about the dangers of being homeless with children in tow. One of the mothers, Sarah, from Sierra Leone was forced from her home during a rebel invasion. Sarah's baby was ripped from her arms and murdered in front of her. The atrocities they have lived through put our problems in perspective. These two African now American mothers, Josephine and Sarah, began to comfort her and talk with her about this baby's condition and what might be done.

"In Africa, we would never let a baby live on the streets," Sarah said. "He would be taken to an auntie or a cousin. Someone would take him in. I don't understand how we let this happen here in America. It doesn't make any sense to me."

The three of us were standing around the young mother who was sitting in the pew, trying to comfort her and come up with a solution. I shook my head. "I guess in America, we are a different kind of village. We have to have the system step in, if we call DCS, the baby will be taken into state custody and then put into the foster care system, it's not guaranteed that the baby will have one home, it may have many in that system, it's not perfect, it's just the system we have, but it does often work out in favor of the child's safety."

"I just want to take him home," the young mother said. "I want to feed him and bathe him and make sure he feels safe. It's killing me that he's not."

"We have to do something," Josephine said. "We can't just let these babies live on the streets, we have to intervene."

The women reasoned through the situation and decided that we should, as a church, call DCS. The only problem: there was no way to locate the couple, and she was expecting another child, due in two weeks.

The next community meal, the couple did not show up. Perhaps they intuitively knew something was going to happen. I haven't seen them since, and as I asked around—no one knew where they went. I had no words of comfort for the young mother. Only, that these are just the kinds of situations we encounter when we do this type of work. It's hard, but sometimes all we can really do is pray and keep searching for some kind of miraculous solution, giving what we can give, doing what we can do while we wait. Sometimes, even I have a hard time heeding this advice because my heart breaks, too.

I grew up in a very small town. In a small town, there is a culture of remembrance. People remember your personality—the things that made you unique—and your family. There is a deep well of recognition. Even in this day and age, there are no homeless people in my hometown.

But in the city, people fall through the cracks. I don't know where they go. There are places to hide, even in plain sight, where no one will ever find you. It haunts me just like it haunted this young mother that a baby did not have what it needed to survive, that a little one so tender could be at risk in a great big world. This precious, new life, in danger of slipping through the cracks.

As an urban pastor, I've tried to create a culture of remembrance, but it's hard because sometimes I feel as if my one, precious life is slipping through the cracks, too. There is something exciting about being in a city with its opportunities, but if you are from a culture of remembrance, it's difficult to stay in that forgotten place.

I often admire the African refugees in my church because they stick together. They are surrounded by their culture here in the city. Even though they joke with me that they have "left the village behind" to fit into the urban culture, this is not really true. The village lives inside of them like my hometown lives inside of me. It guides them to take care of their neighbors' children, to look out for one another, to be kind, and to protect the vulnerable. They have always carried the village in their hearts and as long as they do, they will never feel lonely.

I've learned so much from them and they have become the very heart beat of my church and ministry here, they have so much to teach us about how to love. They are so grateful to be living in what they call a "great country," free from the kind of violence that drove them from their homeland. Here, they can use their gifts, pursue their humble dreams, educate their children, and make a life for themselves. And yet, they do not understand why we have so many holy, homeless families.

I'm not sure what will happen to the holy, homeless family but I pray for their safety and for the well-being of the babies. I pray for a new world in which we cherish all the sacred, holy families in our communities. I have learned that the only home we truly have is the one that is carried in the hearts of others.

3. Corona and the Broken Church

Monday morning, and once again, I avoid tripping over the three-inch elevated flaw in the concrete sidewalk in front of the church where the earth has pushed up the corner.

"I need to get that fixed," I utter beneath my breath, letting the guilt rise in me that I haven't done it yet.

I then torture myself with a scenario I am certain will happen: an elderly person will be looking over their left shoulder at those two giant cornerstones into which the dates 1889 and 1956 are skillfully carved (placards to the banner years) and suddenly remember their baptism or their wedding in this church, unconsciously take a step forward, and tumble. In my mind, this has already happened at least twenty times so if there is such a thing as self- fulfilling prophecy, I apologize in advance to those who are injured upon attempting to enter this church. I apologize for tarnishing your nostalgia, because despite my best efforts and my youngest, most energetic years, I have not been able to make the entrance stable.

I glance at the railing, knocked out of its base several years ago and made wobbly because a truck had backed in to unload supplies for a birthday party rental of the fellowship hall. It was a quinceañera, a very large party with lots of Corona. The clause in the building usage permit says in Spanish, "No alcohol on the premises," but even though it was translated, it was not comprehended. I stopped by at the beginning of the party to ask the five men who were exactly five inches shorter than me to open the five coolers on the kitchen floor for my inspection, having cited the evidence of cardboard Corona boxes in the alley. I said that I was concerned that they might not be in compliance with our policy. Even though upon opening the coolers, revealing at least a hundred bottles of Corona, they still denied it was there. I told them they would have to let me watch them remove it from the premises. But, of course, the joke was on me.

    I know this because I stopped by again later and around the kitchen island were standing several men cooking a big pot of posole, a traditional, Mexican soup, and they were laughing and drinking Corona. At this point, I decided that I would give up my battle against Corona, which seemed to be a battle against happiness itself, because half of these men were shaking in fear that I would call the police who would then check their conspicuously missing IDs. Half of the party goers were daring me to walk further in because they had nothing to lay claim to in this world except their *machismo*.

    It was then that something like compassion (or fear) took over because I, too, once liked the taste of Corona, especially with a little lime. The truth is, I envied their party and there was a pang of loneliness in me because I could not participate and had been forced into the role of disrespected den mother, even though we were all about the same age. I was also beginning to understand the lives of the undocumented in our country and developing a new and profound respect for their capacity for pure joy.

So, the railing got busted that night.

It's been two years since that party, and no one has really noticed the wobbly rail, there are just too many other things to fix.

As usual, the front steps are littered with McDonald's cups, wadded up toilet paper wet from last night's rain, and empty liquor bottles. I go get plastic gloves and remove the debris for another day. (Sometimes I walk past it—just being honest here—and it is secretly removed by someone else. This is grace.)

I have strategically placed incense and Glade plug-ins all around the church to rid that "old smell" every time you open the door. Some kind soul planted pink and red Knock Out roses all around the perimeter. I prune them regularly and bring them inside.

The work is beginning for the day. Downstairs, an agency begins its daily pace of working with refugees and their children, mostly from Africa. There is laughter in the hallways, women dressed in saris with their babies heaped up on their backs, and men dressed nicely for citizenship classes. The bathroom doors slam a hundred or more times in one day (I need to get that fixed, too).

I pick up the tissues that overflow in the trash can. I am the pastor, and yet, I feel invisible.

Another agency that works with families of prisoners and a psychologist who sees clients will have their people in, the doorbell right beside my office will ring for them at least fifteen or more times. I am pleased that they are thriving. In the beginning, they were also like those refugees, lost.

In the other basement, on the other side of the building, a very passionate woman runs a food pantry—she has found her place. Here, in the church, it's become a close-knit community for those who are on the streets. Sometimes the homeless lay on the tattered couches in a dead sleep like seals beaten by angry waves.

I have invited them all into this building to grow, to be, to do the work of Christ in a place that time has almost forgotten. Everyone seems to be thriving around a church that is struggling to be—everyone but me, that is. During the week, I feel forgotten, like the church itself. Though there is music, I blend with ghosts. Though I know I am full, I feel hollow. I remind myself of a beautiful Hafiz poem that tells me "I am a hole in a flute that Christ's breath moves through."[iii]

Sunday morning brings a mixture of people, always the fresh-eyed, young adult visitors from the re-gentrifying neighborhood who will come only once or twice and move on to the larger church down the street with so much more to offer in the way of emotional satisfaction, or they will just give up completely. It's a mystery, what they desire; even with my leftover rock-and-roll persona, I am not hip enough to figure it out. Critical mass, they say, is what's missing. People want to feel comfortable and anonymous, not on display. I get it, I want that, too, sometimes. We just don't satisfy that criterion, perhaps.

The faithful few, those who are on a spiritual journey, those who support and are fed by the uniqueness of this particular haven, come together. The wonderful, bright group of educators, professionals, activists, writers, editors, students, musicians, workers in the world, and the homeless, too. They come together. I love them, I love the light they bring, and no matter how much statistics state the few numbers do not warrant me being their full- time pastor, I still say to those faithful few that they are enough.

I'm getting ready to take on another church, part time, just down the street, to make ends meet for both congregations. It's just where we're at in our time, struggling to be the church.

I know of no magic formula. I only know that there is a violence in the world that often seems so much bigger than me. I pick up the trash it leaves behind and I ask God to intervene. I am not sheltered from it, though I have a thin veneer of insulation, I see it. I try and open some portal in the universe for God's intervention to happen. Each Sunday, I break the bread and I say, "Take and eat, this is my body, broken for you, as often as you do this, remember me." We eat it, the ones gathered. We put our offerings in the plate. We believe we are all here for a purpose greater than ourselves, though the evidence is shaky, depending on the day.

There is a violence in the world and I feel its reverberations every day, the people who come through the doors are beaten in its wake. The Pope said the church is a triage hospital on the front lines of the world's dystopia, though he didn't use the word dystopia, he used "pain."

   As much as I would like to lead another life, one where I am rewarded for my accomplishments, I keep returning to the facts as I cannot help but see them, a darkening spirit in our world.

   These days, I don't do more, I pray more.

   I am a female pastor in a time when the world's violence against the feminine is so engrained in our psyche that we even do it to ourselves. I don't know how to rise above it, other than becoming aware of it and letting it pass through me each day which is healthier than denying it is there. Asking God to heal me, at least enough to become an authentic person when everything is pushing me to be something else. This is an act of defiance each day, stepping over the step that is actually a flaw, shaking off the air of destitution and the pain of utter loneliness to be, for another day, grateful. It goes against every bone in my body, but it is what I know must be done each day, at my altar, surrender.

   Love is the most powerful force in the universe still, and I bow before it, knowing it is my only hope of salvation.

   Some days, this is the greatest act I can do and it is enough.

4. The Rock of a Thousand Flaming Arrows

"Can I talk to you in private for about five minutes?" Nick, a formerly homeless man in his 40s who just moved into an apartment last week, asked me at our church's community meal.

Although he had spent the last two years living in his truck and suffering the usual street life trauma, theft, occasional beating while defending his turf, being hospitalized, in addition to having a disease that causes his hands to violently tremor, it would be perfectly normal for him to request aid from me. But even though he's been living on the edge of utter hell, he never wants to talk to me about any of that. He only wants my opinion on one thing. God. He's been reading through the Bible and he always has questions along with a few fascinating stories.

Nick is perfectly sane, I might add, which is a miracle. Yes, he has the stress and strain of living on the streets, and his hands shake so much from his disease that he can't hold his food or drink without spilling it all over himself, but his mind is intact. So when he speaks of what he calls his strange and mysterious experiences of God, I always give him exquisite attention.

"There's just no other way to describe the things that happen to me, and it really freaks me out. I mean, why does God think so much of me? I'm nobody." He held his hands together in the air to keep them from shaking to emphasize his point.

This is his usual warm up for what he is about to tell me. I'm not sure why he chose me as his confessor of mystical events; maybe it's because I believe him. I believe him because his experiences are true for him and that's enough for me.

I invited him to walk back to the small chapel downstairs so we could chat for a few minutes beyond the noise of the meal. He began his story about a young woman who visited with him while he was sitting in his usual spot in the park across the street from the church. "She was in her 20s," he said, "with very long, multi-colored, finely woven dreadlocks. She was beautiful. She was so bright and clean and wearing very nice clothes. She had a glowing light all around her. Her car was high end and brand new as if she had just driven it off the lot. She told me everything about my life, and then she encouraged me, she said I just needed to hang in there until I can get into an apartment, that it's going to happen."

It had been a long journey to get Nick into an apartment. Massive amounts of paperwork that he refused to do for months, several agencies working together tirelessly to make it happen, and starting a Go Fund Me campaign. Months later, he was about to move in, but the move-in date kept getting postponed every week.

His eyes were gleaming as he spoke. "After we talked for about an hour, she told me she had something to give me, she looked in her pockets, in the back seat and trunk of her car, in the glove box, she couldn't remember where she put it, and then she finally pulled, out of nowhere, a rock shaped like a heart and placed it in my hand. She said she found it when she was having a hard time and I needed to hold on to it because I would need it. Then she drove away. Do you think she was an angel?"

"I don't know," I said, "but I do believe God walks the earth in human skin."

Then he went out to his truck and retrieved a heart-shaped rock that was the size of the palm of his hand. He handed it to me, and it looked as if it had been chiseled by water, so shiny, tan, and flat.

I held it in my hand and tried to imagine her giving it to him. I visualized the beauty of that exchange as I stroked the smooth stone. From the corner of my eye, I could tell he was observing me closely as I admired it. When I handed it back to him, he held up his hands to refuse and offered it to me as a gift. But I insisted he take it back.

I said, "If she told you that you need to keep it, and she might have been an angel, like you say, I would take that kind of thing seriously." I winked as he opened his hands exactly as people do when they are receiving communion, palms up in reverence and surrender. I placed the stone gently into the cusp of his palms.

"You're right," he said, "I better hold on to it," and he slipped it into his front pocket.

A few weeks later, again, we sat down in the small chapel, with the last bit of the day's sunlight streaming through the stained glass windows, along with the sounds of heavy traffic and sirens from the busy street. Nick began to unravel another sacred tale. He told me he wanted to know my opinion of a dream he had the night before.

Having kept a dream journal for the past two years, and having had so many vivid dreams myself, I was very intrigued and ready to listen.

Nick recalled his dream: "I was caught in the middle of two ancient armies with chariots and swords, they were in a war and I was in the middle, it was total chaos. I was fleeing for my life and all of the sudden I saw God up ahead of me. I called out to Him to help me and He came to me and placed a rock in my hand. He told me to ask whatever I wanted from this rock and it would come to pass. So I asked a thousand flaming arrows to come out of the rock, and they did, one by one, and protected me. Then I woke up. What does it mean?"

I said, "I have no idea and I don't really interpret dreams, but if I were to just react to your dream I would say that it seems you are having a lot of anxiety about this new transition in your life, moving into a safe place after having been out in the craziness of the streets, just surviving, for a very long time. Maybe the rock symbolizes your life, that you feel you've been given a gift from God. Maybe you are not sure what to do with this new life you've been given, this precious gift."

"Yeah, maybe you're right," he said. "I don't really know how to take all the kindness coming my way right now. My apartment has been completely furnished by people I don't even know, everything is bought for me. I have money; I really don't know how to take it all in, and I don't feel I deserve it."

In his former life, Nick had everything. A big house, a sports car, plenty of money—until he got the disease and lost his job. But the past two years since he had been on the streets, he discovered something that none of that provided, a mysterious presence of God in the world, provision that he did not have to strive for, a kind of peace he had never known before. He made it his mission to use his one possession, his truck, to redistribute food gleaned from grocery stores, farmer's markets, and local food pantries to all the homeless in the city who couldn't find food sources on their own. It became his mission to deliver food to camps hidden in the woods on the outskirts of the city, to people living under bridges or in their cars, to the homeless, hidden ones among us. Some say there are as many as 25,000 hidden ones in our city. In his mission to the hidden, he sees God everywhere. "Maybe this is where God is hiding," he often says, "with the people who need Him the most."

Nick has never been without money or food. Random people come up to him all the time and give him money, food, and gifts, and say things to him that he feels are messages straight from heaven. Every Thursday he has a new story for me of strange and wonderful occurrences he simply cannot explain.

I always tell him the same thing: "When God gives a gift, both the giver and the receiver are confused."

It's a holy confusion, I tell him, a spiritual thing. We don't always understand or comprehend God's giving, we just receive it with awe and wonder, and it changes us, it alters our path, it makes us real.

I reminded him how lucky he was to have been given such a clear vision of his life. First the heart-shaped rock from the mysterious stranger and now the rock in his dream. "God has a purpose for your life," I said, "and it's going to be amazing."

His story reminded me of the rock at Horeb, the one Moses tapped with his staff to make the water pour out and quench the thirst of the Israelites and their livestock. Having been recently freed from generations of slavery, they did not yet possess the skills to navigate a life of freedom. The fact that the wilderness held valuable resources was a reality that was lost to them.

God gave them a rock too. But it meant nothing to them at first, the gifts of the rock would only be revealed through the stubbornness of prayer. But they were just learning how to be free, and trusting that their resources would be provided was counter intuitive at first. When they were lost and thirsty and felt as if they were going to perish, they used the coping skills they had learned in a life of captivity; complaining, arguing, blaming their leaders. These were the skills that helped them survive a life of slavery. They didn't let go of them easily.

However, as Moses taught them, they wouldn't be able to see the resources hidden inside the rock or have access to them without first letting go of some of their old ways of thinking.

Not only did they not possess the skills to access the resources of the rock, they simply could not imagine that their provision would be given without struggle. They were stuck in trauma syndrome thinking, filled with self-doubt and negative thoughts, still anticipating the crack of Pharaoh's whip. In the throes of this emotional conflict, they just couldn't stop arguing and getting angry at their leader, Moses. They had gone from being physically enslaved to a kind of mental and emotional enslavement. So Moses and Aaron led by example, they escaped the chaos of the arguing, bickering and blaming and went into the quiet and protection of the sacred tent of meeting to pray to God about the crisis at hand.

As they prayed, God showed them that this sacred rock placed in their pathway, the rock at Horeb, was full of life, full of living water, and told them how to access it. Moses tapped it with his staff and water poured out freely for everyone to drink.

In the Old Testament, rocks are often used as a motif that signifies the sacred and holy. Rocks are associated with God, refuge, and life, a sacred place where the soul can find shelter. In the New Testament, the foundation of the Christ community is an actual person who is referred to as a rock. The rock that holds the presence of God is human life.

Maybe our lives are like this sacred rock given by God, full of resources and provision that have been stored up for our wilderness journey. Maybe all of us are terrified that we will not know what to ask of our lives. Maybe we have a hard time getting out of a chaotic or argumentative environment, feeling like a victim or blaming someone else for our predicament. Maybe we just don't know what to do with our one precious life.

Sometimes it takes a wilderness journey to come to see that what we truly need has been in our hearts all along. Sometimes we have to be made uncomfortable so that we can look beyond our comfort zone and dig more deeply for the life we so desperately need. Sometimes we need angels in human skin to point the way, to put a heart-shaped stone in our hands, and tell us that we will certainly need it someday.

For each of us there is a desert, a wilderness journey. Somehow we have to cross a great boundary before we can come to discover the resources we have inside of us, given to us as the gift of creation, the image of God within.

For Nick, it was two years of being homeless.

For others, it may be loss or sickness or a traumatic journey. It's important to know we can all channel our inner Moses, our inner prophet. We can go to a sacred place, become quiet and pray to God. We will find there that we are already known by God and we have already been given what we need. Sometimes the resources we feel we may never find are right in front of us, and all we need is faith and prayer to be given the eyes to see them. We can escape the chaos of our lives and slip into the sacred space of prayer and ask God where and how to find the resources for our lives to truly be of service to a greater good. These are the kinds of navigation skills that lead each of us to a promised land, a soul home, the place where the rock of our lives pours its gifts freely for the greater good.

5. It's Time to Call the Experts

Another manic Monday began with a few rapid texts to other pastors in the area, to locate a pall (a cloth spread over a coffin). I'm not sure I knew exactly what a pall looked like until today.

While those texts continued in rapid fire fashion—simultaneously, I had the following things happening in the building: a funeral visitation with a casket and a hundred beautiful flowers in the sanctuary; Asian refugees with children getting resettled in the church basement with occasional train forays to the bathroom upstairs; a community group potluck and slide show presentation in the fellowship hall; Spanish lessons in the back office; a therapy session in the middle office (and what else?) Oh yeah, key electronic devices breaking down.

I have come to see this as normal. *Sigh.* The day is closing and I can say that it was good. (Oh, death where is thy sting, oh grave, where is thy victory?)

Sometimes decisions are easy, like throwing away the five tubs of potato salad brought in for the grieving family that had exceeded its bad bacteria window by about four hours.

However, I often feel as if I'm in perpetual training mode. For example, I had no idea that a six-hour funeral visitation was considered long. Learning to pace myself, it's a new thing. But somehow, because I was willing to be present, I was graced with a beautiful conversation with a (very old) lifelong Baptist minister, beloved by the community. He and I were to do the funeral together. He had been the pastor of the First Baptist Church just a block down the road for 30-plus years. We began chatting and I said, "That was a good-sized church, I have heard."

He said, "Yes, at one time we had five thousand members."

I shook my head. "I can't imagine that."

To which he replied, "It was hard for me to imagine, too, it was *very* hard."

I knew what he meant. I was keeping a small flock of people going with a large footprint of ministry, it was difficult to imagine meeting the needs of thousands, but somehow, he survived. I knew the so called "glory days" of that church were, like this church, a thing of the past. But that never mattered to me, especially today when there was just so much to be done, and vitality had taken on a new frame, at least for the moment.

The Baptist pastor and I sat down and planned the funeral service, and afterward, he asked me to pray for people who had gathered to pay their respects to the elderly woman who had passed away. Over her lifetime, she had held memberships in both the Methodist church and the Baptist church. So, we were to split the duties. I was relieved that he had taken charge. I obliged the prayer and on his way out, he shook hands with the family and invited them to his revival. He was genuinely smooth. I had so much to learn.

The pressing in of those who come to pay homage to the dead in a church is an honest and somber thing.

Before they came, I surveyed the rickety railing out front that needed to be stabilized, the yoga gear, and leftover Taize candles that needed to be picked up off the chapel floor, the holes and scuff marks on the walls, the cobwebs in the corners, the grape juice stains on the carpet. What did I see, really, but evidence of the living? Why should I be concerned about that? When people fill a room with their respect and gentle conversation, those blemishes fade and are made perfect in the long ray of late afternoon sun beaming through the stained-glass window.

    Sometimes in this vocation, I'm able to linger and hover in that space between the living and the dead. I never get to choose when this happens. Today was such a day. No, I am not being sentimental. It's a true and honest moment in which all the collective humanity and all the invading Divine kiss one another.

    In life and death, one has something to give, and another has something to take in the inevitable exchange. Here, I will give you a mother and someday, you will give her back. Here, I will give you a child, and there is no guarantee that this precious gift will last a lifetime. You cling, but you must eventually let go. You want to follow but you must stop short and let her go. You must watch as the adult son watches the beautician lovingly curl his mother's hair in the soft, satin folds of the coffin. You must accept that this is the very last day he will touch her skin.

    At the end of the day, I took the remaining food to the industrial fridge. The digital thermometer read 88 degrees. It was about the third major electronic product to fail in one day.

How strange. Should I call the electrician?

I hadn't had time to call the repair tech for the copier or the internet service provider—come to think of it, the phone had not rung all day— and then there was that two-hour period where my Finance Chair had unintentionally locked me out of my office after counting yesterday's offering . . . nah, it was already eight o'clock at night.

I pulled the refrigerator plug out of the wall, turned out the lights, and decided to save it for tomorrow morning, at which point I would call in the experts.

6. You Can't Play a Player

"I came to Nashville as a tramp," he said. He was just another guy in the crowd of many who come from the streets to our weekly meal.

I eventually learned his name, it was Charles, and began calling him something other than "tramp."

"Gossip on the street is that Nashville is tramp friendly," Charles said.

Charles had come here from the deep South to make a go of it, but explained that as he made his way to the many churches that offered aid, he observed that "tramps" like him were just taking advantage of everyone's kindness and not trying to get better or get off the streets. He discovered how easy it was to become complacent and just live off the goodwill of others.

Although I would never put the words "complacent" and "homeless" together in a sentence, this was his story, not mine.

He was troubled that he rarely experienced a homeless person taking the hard steps toward becoming self-sufficient. He explained this was why he had a hard time getting motivated to get off the streets.

I pointed out to him that his philosophical nature was a very good quality, albeit, a tortuous one. He went on to pontificate that this realization made him question whether having these free services for the homeless was a good thing.

"Doesn't it just make the problem worse?" he asked. He also said that it seemed really condescending from his perspective, that churches would just offer meals and assistance without ever really getting to know people or trying to change the problems. Basically, in his opinion, churches were just being played by the "tramp" community in Nashville and it was disturbing to him, though, he was deeply appreciative. He said, "Don't get me wrong." I assured him that I would never.

Charles had a great point. You've most likely heard the paraphrase, from some cobweb deep in one of the prophetic books of the Old Testament, "Charity gives but justice changes." This is what he was referring to. He didn't see any real change happening around him, he only saw charity, not justice. He thought we were all engaged in a giant game of blowing smoke, and because we were only committed to charity—not the harder work of justice—we were vulnerable to being played by the players, like himself.

I reminded him that "being played" tends to be a casualty in the compassion business. It's not what we set out to do and, of course, it's great when we can avoid it. But, as it happens, even Jesus was played by Judas, and instead of stopping it, he let the whole deathly thing unfold. We don't get involved with acts of compassion to avoid being played, we get involved serving others so that some people, a few people, can recognize what it means to receive love with no strings attached, and they can choose to be changed by it. Perhaps the numbers won't be great. Perhaps we won't solve homelessness in our community. Jesus never fixed the problem of poverty in his day, but he gave us the tools to heal one another. Healing is the very first step in any process that holds any meaning at all.

When we give a meal, or learn someone's name, or take someone to Target to buy them underwear, we are doing what we can in the moment that heals. This leads people to decide if they want to apply for food stamps or apply for housing, something they had not done before and were living in a state of despair because they thought no one cared. Small acts of healing add up over time and then gives people the courage to trust again, to become part of a small support group that deals with issues of addiction and recovery to risk becoming part of a community. This leads them to search for a part-time job; maybe it's washing cars or cleaning out gutters, but the point is that it leads them to clean themselves up and apply for life again. We can't just tell a person, who has been rejected from the human community, to just "go out and get a job." Applying for a job means that they actually trust that there is some system out there that cares about them. We have to heal rejected people first. We have to do something as significant as looking honestly into the eyes and hearts of all those who have been turned away by society and have the courage to hold a steady gaze. We have to restore their trust in humanity. This usually happens gradually with several communities and several people touching one person's life.

What I have come to realize as I work in the community of the disenfranchised and downtrodden is the only difference between me and the ones I am trying to help is that they have been disconnected, at some critical juncture in their lives, rejected, from the framework that was supposed to give them life. They did not have the resources, as I did, to keep them off the streets. The streets became their home, not by choice, but by necessity. They have become players because it's how they survive, it's how they live.

When I began working with the homeless community, I realized, over time, that because of my encounters with them, I became a different kind of player. I no longer cared about the things I worried about so much in my former life. Status, success or failure, the fear of having or not having, these worries began to leave me. As I began to feel free from these burdens, I experienced the joy of true connection with others. I no longer viewed people as stepping stones and I became freer to express love and to risk vulnerability by serving others.

The nature of God awaits all of us each time we offer ourselves in service of another (with safety precautions, of course) without an agenda or outcome in mind, without judgment, just allowing God to be present between us. In this state of mind, played or not played, it really doesn't matter. The joy that is given in the holy exchange is more precious than gold.

7. It's Hard to Know Exactly What to Do

I am a lighthouse keeper. At least, this is what I tell myself on those nights when I'd much rather stay inside rather than walk from the parsonage to the church building to close it down for the night. Each evening, I have a routine. My perky yellow lab Sophie and I walk through the dark halls of the church, mostly empty by nightfall. I turn off the lights, adjust the thermostats, and fasten the large, creaky metal gates to the parking lot. Occasionally, I meet a surprise.

The surprise came in the form of a human being, lying on his side, half on the church parking lot and half in my yard. He looked terribly uncomfortable.

I hesitated because I don't normally just walk up to strangers on the property at night, living as I do next to a busy street and casually say "Hey, what brings you here?" Urban life requires a different kind of vigilance than living in a small town.

But the dilemma was that he was in my yard, and I had to walk across his path to get to the door of the parsonage.

So, I put on my best authority voice and yelled from a safe distance, "Hey, what's going on?"

He mumbled something, leaned up on one elbow. "You're the pastor lady?"

I noticed he had taken off his shoes and was trying to air dry his socks by laying them out neatly on the grass. I asked him, "What are you doing laying in my yard?"

"Can you give me a ride?"

I paused for a moment. "...and your name is?"

"Darin. Can you give me a ride?"

"Uh, no. I don't give rides to strange men I've just met, but I can give you bus fare. Where are you going?"

He shuffled on his feet a bit. "Oh, I left my backpack, my ID, everything, down that way." He pointed west. "It's on a hill I think it's three or four miles."

"A hill," I said. "Um, do you know what's near the hill?"

"No—" he looked down at his feet— "I don't remember."

He had nothing, no possessions, no money, no wallet just the clothes on his back. He didn't know where he had come from and refused my offer of bus fare, to get on a bus to nowhere. I suppose I couldn't blame him. Buses can only take you somewhere if you have a destination in mind.

I wasn't sure what to do for him, but noticed he was perfectly sober which was (not to sound crass) kind of rare in these cases.

He grew increasingly frustrated as I was unable to comply with his idea of what needed to happen and finally convinced me he needed $30 for the night, so I gave him the money and told him to come back the next morning. We would try and sort out a solution for his missing ID.

He returned the next morning.

I asked him what he had done with the money, certain he had spent it on alcohol.

He pulled the crumpled receipt out of the front pocket of his jeans, pressed it out slowly in the palms of his hands and gave it to me. He wanted me to see that he had been industrious with his money. He had bought a new pair of shoes, two pair of socks, a sweatshirt, and cigarettes.

"This sweatshirt is really nice," he said excitedly, taking it out of the plastic bag to show me. "You should feel it, you should maybe get this for your husband. It was only $8. These shoes aren't any good, though," he said, lifting up one foot to show me where one of the seams around the sole of the shoe had already ripped. "I went back to the store to get my money back, but they threw me out. I guess $30 doesn't go very far anymore."

I was amazed at how honest and wise he had been with the money. This, too, was rather rare.

As I chatted with him I noticed that he had the feel of someone who had been taken care of at one time, someone with a family. He lacked the hard edges in his face and eyes, and he did not yet have the cower, the detached, glassy stare that most homeless people possess that tells you the hope of being the recipient of human warmth has left their hearts. He didn't seem to drink alcohol, either. He seemed to be free from that nameless condition produced by rejection, abandonment, and abuse that has strickened most of the homeless people I meet. Rather, he had a look that said "I expect you to give me warm milk, read me a bedtime story, and tuck me in." It seemed he felt entitled to be in my yard, even though he was only halfway committed. He seemed like someone who was loved but very lost.

He still insisted that I drive him to the unknown hill where he left his possessions, even though he had no idea where that hill was.

I explained—again—that it wasn't my policy to give anyone rides, but I could still give him bus fare. (My friend who binge watches Netflix forensic detective shows tells me, "Don't ever, ever do that. That's how nice women end up in pieces in barrels.") Of course, I wouldn't do that, but I did need to find a way to help him. I've helped enough people over these last ten years I've developed a sense that's second nature. It's a keen awareness of the kind of malady that has brought a person to my door.

In Darin's case, it seemed there was a mental disability. The first clue: he lay on my lawn as if he were home. Most homeless people are so accustomed to being chased away by the world that they don't dare invade personal space. But Darin was different, it was not that he couldn't accept the rejection he'd experienced, he just simply didn't understand it.

He said he was hungry and asked to eat—again—as a child would ask to eat. Perfectly expecting that I would reach in my cabinets and produce something magical for him to eat.

I said I would give him something and we would talk about his situation, but he needed to wait for me while I went inside to turn off my stove.

I went in, turned off the stove where lunch was cooking, and sat down on my couch to pray. I didn't know what to do for him. I prayed for God to show me how to help him. I've learned rushing into situations with frustrated action thinking I could help someone does more harm than good. So praying helps me pause and have the chance of actually helping.

I didn't hear any answers, so I went out to ask him if he had a plan, since he wasn't able to find his ID.

"A plan." He paused. "That's a good question. Usually my Mom helps me think through these things."

I was shocked. "You have a mother? Is she alive?"

"Yes." He rolled his eyes upward as if to say, of course, how could you not know this?

"She lives in Wisconsin." He stuttered a little bit. "She—she—she usually helps me when I get lost." God had given me the answer. I would try to get him home.

"Do you remember her number?"

He remembered three numbers for both parents. He had them memorized, and they were still alive and well.

I invited him into the church kitchen where I opened two cans of beef stew, heated it up quickly in the microwave and gave it to him. As he ate, I called his mother on my cell phone.

Her mature voice was soft and exasperated. She was in shock to receive a call from someone about her son. She immediately wanted to know what every mother wants to know right away, in hurried sentences, she asked me. "Is he okay, does he have clothes, does he have food, where is he staying?"

She explained that over the course of several years, they had tried many things. Sending bus tickets for him to come home but he always got off about an hour into the ride. They had come in person to retrieve him in a few different states, but as soon as he got home, he left again. He was now in his forties. They had spent the past few decades trying to come up with a solution and it seemed as if there was little hope for one.

I asked if she would email me his birth certificate, and we exchanged contact information. His mother did not know what to do now. Her heart hurt for her lost son and there was nothing she could do but send this birth certificate all over the country, time and time again, because he continued to loose his poof of identity.

After the phone call, he asked to wash his hands. I pointed him to the large, industrial sink. As I was cleaning up, he took off his shirt and immersed his entire upper body under the faucet, with dishwashing soap, washed his head and neck and arms, as much as he could cover without getting completely naked. Instead of getting upset, I retrieved a large towel from the bin and handed it to him to dry off.

"You're the only minister who's ever helped me," he said. "Most people just brush me off; it's weird. But you took the time to help me. People don't have time anymore to help people."

This is the moment, another moment in a ten-year series of several, where I feel I am in the presence of yet another angel, yet another sacred unveiling, when I feel the Holy brush between us. *Enough, already. I get it.*

As we sat together at the table in the fellowship hall, I gently explained to him that I understood why he didn't want to go home because he didn't want to take the medicine he needed to have a sane life. "But it's really the best place for you." I said as gently as I could. "You can have hot meals, a warm bed, and people who love and care for you."

"You're probably right," he said as he folded his arms as if to comfort himself, "I probably do need to go home."

I went upstairs and got him a new backpack, one that was imprinted in bright orange letters "UT Vols," left over from our back to school blessing of the backpacks.

He stuffed his $30 worth of belongings in and went off to look for his missing ID. He would be back later, he said, to retrieve his birth certificate and be on his way.

I grabbed a pair of Nikes in the discard pile from my husband's closet, conveniently his size, printed out his birth certificate and glanced at the information filling the nice, neat boxes. This grown man, a perfect stranger, had been a baby once, tender and new. Reading his parent's names, the year of his birth, the hospital where he was born, I thought of the hope of babies, the hope for newness, happiness and life.

I put it in an envelope, wrapped the shoes in a plastic bag and attached it to the door with a note with his name on it.

The envelope and bag disappeared. I hoped he had made it back home. But that wasn't the case. For the next four weeks, Darin would appear and disappear, we would call his Mom, he would get frustrated because the negotiations didn't suit him, and then run away. This went on for weeks. I would sometimes find him asleep on the front steps of the church or hiding in the bathroom. Something inside me said he'd finally make the decision on his own to go home, just give him time.

In the meantime, he found resources: he had a small check coming in from social security so he could buy supplies for camping out in the little thickets of woods that surrounded the outlying areas of the city.

The next time I spoke to his Mom, she asked me how he was, how he looked. "Was he nice to you? I know I'm being negative. I just can't help it, we just don't know what to do and nothing seems to help."

I assured her there wasn't much she could do but keep her boundaries, insisting he take his medication, while holding out the invitation she could not help but make which was "come home."

Sometimes I stood and listened while he held my mobile phone on speaker and spoke with her—it was heartbreaking. I could hear the pain in her voice, a mother's pain that her son wasn't capable of receiving her love and was wandering the streets refusing her help. It must be a pain like no other.

Sometimes, it's hard to know exactly what to do but I pray for the wisdom to do the next right thing, again and again. Each time I have an encounter like this, it seems to cut a deeper groove into my heart where love breaks through, like a ray of sun streaming into a dark cave. Even though it's hard to know what to do, I believe that offering love changes something greater than either of us. It changes the quantity of love in the world. Without people like Darin coming across my path, how would I ever learn to love? How would I ever know what resides deeply within my own heart?

My life would just be business and distraction without people like Darin. I call them all angels, the sacred homeless walking the earth. If we agree to see them as human beings, slow down and have a human exchange, God will give us the wisdom to do what we can do. In that flash of wisdom, we will have a brush with something sacred and we will be changed.

In my little lighthouse keeper/pastor job, I've come to discover that I don't have to save the world and I certainly won't be able to save another person. Even though I'm technically a professional in the taking-care-of-people field, sometimes I just don't know if I'm doing exactly the right thing. Sometimes there are no immediate answers.

It has become an honor to be the one who stands in the gap, holding a space between despair and hope, becoming the eyes and ears of someone else's home, if only for a moment. These encounters have made me a real human being. As I seek to open my heart to love, with wise boundaries in place, I'm guided by a greater hand.

My hope is that Darin will make it home. That someday there will be more solutions for people like him, as we increasingly see more mentally ill, untreated adults falling through the cracks of society, forced to roam the streets. I don't know what the answer is today, but I have faith that we can all find better solutions if we can commit to some common ground and work together towards the flourishing of all people, especially those who are disadvantaged.

8. Where Your Joy Meets the World's Pain, The Soul Whispers a Dream

Recently, I watched a video of film producer, Steven Spielberg, speak about dreams to a class of graduating seniors. He was encouraging them and gave them some clues about how dreams communicate to us. Not in a loud screaming voice, he explained, but in subtle "whispers"[iv] from within. He was speaking of the idea, to borrow from Joseph Campbell, of "following your bliss." The idea that being courageous enough to follow these subtle, soul whispers can lead you to materialize your unique and special dream.

This is a beautiful thought, but even before I could relish it my mind flashed back to Joe, one of the well-known patrons at the free community meal hosted by the urban church where I serve as pastor. Joe and I spent half an hour together when I accompanied him to get his prescriptions filled after the meal. Since becoming a pastor in an urban area, I've heard stories like his many times—enough to know that just outside the soul's perfectly whispered dream lives the dissonant sound of human suffering.

His story is not uncommon. A 52-year-old man whose life had been largely occupied by the diseases of poverty and lack of opportunity. As an adult, he had been stabbed, shot, imprisoned for crimes he did not commit. His childhood was not much better. He was physically abused as a child, without a stable family, growing up in abject poverty His life had been about survival, it seemed, the opposite of the subtle, soul-whispered dreams.

Still, he said, he believed God had a purpose for his life. He got off the streets and now lives in an apartment. That was a big first step. Though he is still barely making it and living with a roommate addicted to heroin, he hopes to move away to a place of his own soon, so he can get his mind straight and do something to help others. Away from the chaos of living in low rent housing, where drug deals, prostitution, and crime are rampant. He told me he did not understand why God would allow human beings to suffer so much, especially children, and to this, there is no answer. But he longed to do something about it. This was his dream, his mission in life.

I have struggled with the gap between the soul's dreams whispering to us and the vast suffering in our own nation of our brothers and sisters and children going hungry, growing up without opportunity. When the soul whispers its dreams, why does it not echo "for everyone"?

In Native American culture there is the practice of a vision quest. The reason for seeking a vision is so that you might discover the dream God has planted in you. The dream is not just for you, it belongs to the tribe and it belongs to the Great Spirit who has dreamed in advance for everyone's good. The belief is that the dream was given to you—a unique individual—allowing you to express a facet of the whole in your own way so that those around you might also be able to dream.

In our culture, however, we often turn the dream into a commodity and exploit it for profit. We isolate the dream from the tribe and in doing so, we cut ourselves off from the very design of the dream, which is to create connection with others. We chase a dream when perhaps we're really craving a vision. We seek wealth, status and prestige when what we really long for is a sense of belonging.

We often want our dreams to pay off and we can spend a lifetime chasing the gold gleaming on the horizon. It is perfectly normal that we would feel this way. After all, we are often isolated and alone, without a tribe, we are convinced we must fend for ourselves, make our own way in the world, and resolve the questions of our own destiny with our will, might, and a "can do" spirit. But what we truly crave deep down is to belong to something greater than ourselves. However, many of us simply don't know how to belong. We long to feel the deep joy of being loved, to have communion with one another, but are at a loss as to how to achieve this. When we live in a world in which something as holy as a dream, a soul whisper, is turned into a commodity on the marketplace, it's no wonder we get confused as to what constitutes a true dream. If it can't be bought or sold, we often don't understand how to interact with it. But we can learn.

A true dream begins from a sense of belonging and expands from there to include the good and well-being of others.

Frederick Beuchner speaks of that place within us all that is the true dream of God, where we find the angels pointing the way. The place where our deepest joy and gladness makes a connection with the world's deepest pain.[v] Maybe the great dream that God whispers to us all is simply to love and help one another in the unique kind of way that only each of us can. When we are using our gifts to reach out to those in need, we find our belonging, our purpose, and when we open our hearts and realize that our tribe is everyone, this is where we find God calling.

There is a Divine purpose, a vision for every soul in the world. Dreams don't *come* true, they already *are* true. The real work is becoming aligned with the dream God has already dreamed in you. The subtle, soul whisper can be heard by leaning close to the heart of God and asking how your gifts might serve the world's great needs.

Homilies and Meditations

9. A Frosty, White Morning

John 4:1-42

I awoke at 3 a.m. on a frosty, white morning and I could not get back to sleep. Something stirring in my dreams startled me awake and seemed to imply that I should pick up the Gospel of John around chapter four, the story of the Samaritan woman at the well. Since I'm always researching some book of the Bible preparing Sunday's sermon, as Sunday comes with frightening regularity, this wasn't really abnormal, I suppose, but it was strangely clear.

As I read the story, in the bleary tiredness of the 3 a.m. wake-up call from the dream world, I recalled the list of things I needed to do for the day. "Change the church sign" was on the top of the list. The sign read "Let all who are thirsty come." I don't like changing it in the cold. My fingers grow numb handling the clumsy, plastic letters, lifting the frosted, heavy, protective glass, and quite frankly, I grow weary of inventing pithy statements in six words or less, cleverly created to inform the busy world that you are about another business. Even though it's been there a few weeks, it is a timeless saying: "Let all who are thirsty come." If I could stay with this theme, maybe I wouldn't have to change the sign.

After all, that was exactly what Jesus was offering her, the Samaritan woman, the lost woman, the woman going through the incurious motions of her day, the woman fetching water from the well, the foreigner, the forbidden one. Living water. He called it "the gift."

The disciples had left him alone with a woman who had come to a well as alone as a lone gazelle in a kingdom of tigers. Jesus was not even where he was supposed to be, again. He was traveling through the region of Samaria, maybe to avoid the crowds. There had been a long-standing hostility between the Jews and Samaritans. So when he asked a Samaritan woman for a drink of water, at first, it made her indignant. Though Jesus knew full well he could give her the mysterious water called Living, where her insatiable spirit would be quenched, he withheld the offer. Rather, it was he who asked her for a drink. He asked her for the gift that only he could give. With the heat of rivalry in her voice, a rivalry that flowed in her blood, a Bloods and Crips kind of loyalty of one to the hatred of the other, she asked, "How is it that you, a Jew, ask for a drink from me, a Samaritan?"

What came next makes entirely no sense, still, he said it: "If only you knew the gift, you would have known that you could ask me for anything and I would give it. You would know the art of the question, that what I am asking from you is what I am willing to give, only more so ... if only you knew the gift."

It was a new kind of offering, this gift. Different than all the other gifts she had sought with her five husbands plus one lover. She had craved a gift, yet all she could find were takers. His words undid her there, this would be a good and different trade, she knew it in her core wherein a life-long ache had, like a river of tears, sculpted a deep crevasse of emptiness. Still, she had nurtured there, somehow scraped together, a rare jewel of intuition and kept it alive. Now she would spend it on this man, for he had unlocked the chamber within which she had stored this rare strain of intuition with one word. That word was, "Gift."

A slew of questions proceeded from her mouth when the lock gave way, it was only natural, it was all such a new experience, this gift. Why? How? With what tools? Where do you come from? Who are you, anyway? The one question she did not ask was, what do you want from me? She was willing to give whatever it took, though she had not yet played her hand.

In that moment of awareness, when time stood still, she drank of the gift of Living water, which was not done with any utensil known to humankind but in the loop of strangeness between two souls.

The disciples returned, and since time was in fact, standing still, they did not say a word.

The woman, filled with her new life, fled the scene, clutching in her soul her gift. The gift was new life.

As this new life is wont to do, it began to spread like wildfire into the village. She testified to what had happened to her and others came and drank this living water. You see, the invitation is not to think about it or pray about it, but to come and see.

After the event, as the crowds were beginning to press in, his disciples tried to get him to eat some food but he was not quite empty yet. He kept saying, "Lift up your eyes and see that the fields are white for harvest."

Today it was a frosty, white morning.

10. Huldah and the End of the World
   2 Kings 22

It was a well-known fact that no one knew the Bible like my grandmother, Mary. No one was watching her, but we all knew from the evidence that she spent a good amount of time each day looking through her magnifying glass at the stories in the Bible. The gold-leafed pages of her King James Bible had faded to gray and the cowhide edges of the cover were permanently upturned. Here and there, the details came out in plain speak, uncolored, unfiltered—like God to the Hebrews—with an undisputed sense of barb and that familiar combination of compassion and wrath.

Oh, usually, it was in statements to me about my appearance. "Are you ever going to comb your hair?" and "Do you go to work looking like that?" Sometimes, the more prophetic statements emerged, like the one I will never forget while sitting at the site of my first wedding (not at a church). She uttered something like "I don't know why you're doin' this, it ain't gonna last."

Blunt speak, she was known for it. I suppose she learned it from the Bible.

She steered me from the great beyond with her stubborn, steadfast faith, through all my many wanderings; she was my magnetic North Star, always pulling me back to her center of gravity.

Huldah was probably a lot like my grandmother. I can imagine her looking up from a careful reading, pointing her magnifying glass at the gang of priests sent by King

Josiah to find her. "Tell that man—" and refusing to say his name— "who sent you to me . . . thus says the Lord God of Israel, thus says the Lord, I will certainly bring disaster on this place." Ouch.

The priests in the presence of Huldah probably felt a lot like I did sometimes in the shadow of my grandmother, shaking from the dread of the implied doom her words often prophesied (which felt mostly like the fear of God). The end of the world, in her mind, was an option that was always lurking around the corner.

One would think King Josiah chose Huldah to interpret the mysterious scroll found hidden within the walls of the temple over Jeremiah because he was looking for a more compassionate voice, a more nurturing presence. After all, Jeremiah was the "go to" prophet of the times. However, Huldah, much like Jeremiah, was not the coddling type. No, she was the tell-it-to-you-straight type, the one you went to for the unabridged truth, the unfiltered truth, the truth unaltered by peer pressure or political allegiance. Perhaps. The truth is, we really don't know why Josiah chose Huldah that day. We can only speculate.

Whatever the reason is, it doesn't much matter. The story is not really about Huldah, as much as I would like for it to be. After all, I've written an entire series of songs about women of the Old Testament, hoping to find some thread of power that connects to all the ways in which I have felt powerless in my own life. But, the story is not really about Huldah or self-empowerment. We don't even know much about her, although it is pretty impressive that she is known as a prophet in the region of Jerusalem. Still, the story is not about that, though it would make for a great story.

The story is not about me, or my grandmother, or even the great King Josiah. No, the story is really about what connects us together, the voice that is speaking through this forgotten scroll and what it has to say to everyone in a time and place, a kingdom and a world. It is a message for them and for us. It is a story about a truth that cannot be hidden or misplaced, a message so creative that it would speak through the rocks and the trees if the human voice refused to be its vessel. It is the message that was written down in this lost scroll that came to be found by a great man, a king, and a great woman prophet in a time and place so long ago that we have to excavate it even from our text.

It is the message that sees through us, all of us. King Josiah and his great righteous zeal, Huldah and her powerful feminine obscurity; the message that sees through this strange point where I meet them in my attempts to be an effective and powerful female clergy leader while trying to mediate the mysterious voice of God from the often-dying relic of the church pulpit; and it is this message that even sees through my grandmother and her sage-like attempts to bring us all down to the stump of our humble beginnings.

Disaster is always looming, it seems, hovering over us like a flock of hungry crows. To live is to experience some kind of disaster. But to know God in this human experience is to be rescued by the sheer force of love.

It feels good and true and right when we are at last seen by this kind of love, when we are rescued from all the ways we have tried to secure it by our own efforts. When we are seen by this kind of love, we are seen through, as it were, by someone who loves us, a friend, a grandmother, a prophet—we feel that a sort of rescue mission for our soul has been underway all along and we never knew it until that very moment when we understood. In that moment, it doesn't matter if the world ends or if our whole life has been some empty pursuit of prestige, or fame and fortune—all that matters is that we have found the one thing we've searched for all our life.

This is the essence of Huldah's story—and ours, too. Finding the treasure buried inside the walls of our own heart. It is just as Huldah said, when the lost sayings were brought to her. We have to learn, once again, to love with our whole heart if we want to discover the treasure hidden deep within. It is love.

11. A Girl Doesn't Dream of Becoming a Prostitute

Luke 7:36-50; 8:1-3

A girl doesn't grow up dreaming of becoming a prostitute, it's generally a profession born of necessity and driven by an insatiable market demand. In the ancient world when Jesus was around, women who were prostitutes were just called "sinners," a blanket term that covered a multitude of necessary survival traits. Since a woman was considered property, if she was banished or turned out of a home or a marriage, likely with no marketable skills, prostitution became a way of feeding herself—it was survival.

So it is no surprise that, more than once, Jesus found himself in a position where a woman who was a "sinner" hunted him down to kiss his feet and wipe away her tears with her hair, often pouring out some kind of expensive perfume as a gesture that she was laying it all on the line in hope of a new life. Confident that she would get a fair hearing at this man's feet, even if she had to crash a formal "for males only" dinner and parade herself past a table full of men, perhaps even one or two of her former clients. We find in Luke 8:1-3 that Jesus had a cadre of female disciples such as this, former "sinners." These very women he had freed from a life of "sin" (what we might call sex trafficking today), and the accompanying demons and infirmities, ended up providing financial support for his ministry out of their new jobs and their newfound lives as freed women.

Jesus had a group of women funding his mission—women he had set free—which indicates by the nature of the word "free" that prior to their falling at his feet like a refugee of war seeking asylum from an oppressive regime, they had been in a captivity known as sin. Ironically, the label of "sinner" wasn't given to the system that forced a woman into such circumstances or the pimp that ran the prostitution ring rather, the one who bore the label "sinner" was the woman herself.

But Jesus saw the matter differently, instead of blaming the woman for her predicament, he simply set her free, not only from her internal demons and infirmities but from the system itself. He gave her the ability to build a new life. Perhaps Jesus was the first feminist.

At the beginning of his ministry when Jesus states that he has come to set the captives free, he's talking about human beings who are enslaved to systems that force them to live apart from the joy and dignity of their very soul, which is, by the way, a God-given right for every human being.

The guiding energy of any movement such as feminism or liberation is to free people to experience their souls, the God-given source of their true nature. This is what Jesus meant by "free." Freedom to experience the place of connection with God that is often blocked by the psychological trauma that comes with physical, mental and spiritual types of oppression.

Oppressive forces that enslave people by treating them as property are also forces that threaten a person's connection to their very own soul. For the women in these stories, and for so many people in the world today, Jesus becomes a force stronger than the oppressive forces in the world that enslave. Jesus represented God, not just in a building but in the heart, a force that can set the soul free to experience the joy, freedom, peace, and eternal nature of God here and now.

Saint Irenaeus said, "The glory of God is a person fully alive." I'm sure these women of the ancient world became dangerously independent and fully alive when Jesus set them free. Independent enough to make their own living and give themselves to a worthy cause without selling body and soul. As the ancient poet Hafiz has stated, "We have not come here to be taken prisoner, but to surrender ever more deeply to freedom and joy."

Quite a feat in a world in which women were considered the property of another person, subversive, in fact, to believe in something that doesn't technically belong to you, your very self. This is often the first step to the recovery of the soul, believing, against the odds, that you can reclaim your soul from any kind of wreckage that may have been hoisted upon you in this life.

Perhaps the greatest gift Jesus gave women, besides the connection to their soul's divine joy, was the permission to believe in themselves without apology.

12. Learning to Slay the Dragons Within
Judges 5:34-30

Why is true identity so threatening? Take Buffy, the popular female heroine from the hit TV show *Buffy the Vampire Slayer*, for example. When Buffy discovers her true gift, the ability to slay vampires and fight evil, she has a hard time accepting it. But as she grows, develops and utilizes her gift, she learns that she is, in fact, a vampire slayer, as she suspected. As she uses her gift to meet a great need in the world, the destruction of evil, she slowly comes around to accepting her true identity.

Buffy's story moves so many people because we all face such seemingly insurmountable challenges in our day-to-day lives that can feel overwhelming, threatening to our very life force. In her, we see ourselves, confused about our gifts, uncertain as to how we might embrace who we really are and use our unique gifts, somehow, for good in the world. However, as we learn how to let go of our fears, embrace our gifts and move into something that feels true to ourselves, we learn how to become slayers, not of people or vampires, but of the great dragons within us all: fear, anxiety, self-doubt, shame, and the long list of terrifying emotions that threaten to do us in and steal precious energy meant to be used for good. As we grow, we learn to call these dragons by name. As we watch Buffy grow into her calling, we see that it requires an enormous amount of trust in her inner voice to find her way, and there is no shortage of other voices telling her not to listen to her instincts.

This teaching is also at the root of an Old Testament Bible story in which a female slayer from the ancient world, Jael, saved the Israelites from destruction by murdering Sisera, a ruthless and corrupt Canaanite leader. Narrated in Judges 5, Jael's story unfolds as the Israelites incite a rebellion against the Canaanites who had held them as captives for twenty years. Like Deborah, the other powerful woman in this story, the warrior prophet, who led the Israelites into battle, Jael also channeled her warrior power to fight evil. She lured Sisera into her private tent, gave him something soothing to drink, and had him lie down to take a nap. As he was sleeping, she took a hammer and a tent stake and drove it through his skull.

So Buffy-like.

Jael could have been the original Buffy. She is celebrated in Judges as the nomadic woman who tricked Sisera into her tent with her gifts of charm, wit, and beauty. There, she steadied her prey, making him feel relaxed and safe before she went in for the kill.

Was Jael using her God-given gift? Perhaps. It is difficult for us to embrace a story with such violence in a literal manner of interpretation. Rather, if we interact with this story in a similar fashion as we do when we watch *Buffy the Vampire Slayer*, or as if we are listening to a storyteller around a campfire, we might be able to see a bit of ourselves. When we hear this story with awe, wonder, and imagination we see something very different. Not only do we explore a different perspective of women's roles in the Bible, but we can imagine ourselves embracing our own fears and learning how to utilize our unique gifts. The story says, "He sank, he fell, he lay at her feet." Sisera was known for raping and plundering after a victory. "Two women for every man," the story goes. Yet, our heroine prevails. "Blessed is Jael; she slays the dragon; she is fearless and victorious; she is a slayer of the dark."

The journey of faith is often a pathway of learning to connect with your true identity which very often requires some kind of inner journey. At times, our emotions such as fear and anxiety can seem like dragons (or even vampires) threatening to suck the life out of us or harm us in some way. But as we learn to connect with our gifts and have the courage to use them to meet some of the great needs of the world, we begin to develop confidence, self-respect and courage to "slay the dragons within."

As we build this bridge between true identity and the needs of the world, we come to connect with what is true within ourselves, this beautiful image of God within. Sometimes, the story in you is just as hidden as the stories in the Bible. But the story is there, within, sometimes it just requires a little digging.

What I find so amazing about these hidden stories of the Bible is that the narrators left them in, these fearless, courageous women leaders; judges, prophets, slayers. Just like these amazing, hidden stories in the Bible, there is an amazing, hidden story in you, too. As we explore the story written on the walls of our own soul, our true gifts come out of hiding. As our gifts come out and touch the world, we find self-acceptance and learn to slay the dragons within.

The point is, as much as we have tried to domesticate our Bible and domesticate ourselves, there still remains space that is utterly wild and untamed within. Maybe we should take a second look at what we think we know both about Bible and ourselves and toss that knowledge out the window.

The same window where Sisera's mother waits for him in vain. The window where she sits searching the horizon for her son—that dragon, rapist, plunderer—preparing, as she always did, to praise him for his victory. Perhaps it's time to realize that the very window that would seal us in will also set us free.

13. The Gift of the Ashes

Ash Wednesday Meditation

I took a walk this morning with my highly-attuned yellow lab, Sophie, through our Nashville neighborhood, newly frosted with snow, a blank canvas of white, full of possibility. In March, the month of this year's Lent, we hover between winter and spring, between death and resurrection, between waiting and rising. We create a space in our hearts where something old might die and something new might bloom. These were my thoughts as I was walking, but Sophie was oblivious to all of this, she was just hunting squirrels.

Last night's threatening ice had brought the school buses, harried employees late for work, and noise pollution from the interstate to a hush. Robins, cardinals, blue jays, mockingbirds, finches, crows, and blackbirds pierce the air with song as they have come out from their hiding places to search for today's breadcrumbs.

We all yearn for spring, for the thaw, with its fluorescent green and goldenrod. In the doldrums of winter, we are oblivious to spring's surprises, her thunderstorms, and her turbulent tornadoes.

We're living in a new normal. More ice, more snow, more fire, more wind, less rain, and more rain than ever before. Heat will come with summer and hotter than we think we can bear.

The world is a beautiful and terrifying place at the same time, and it is where I belong. I belong to the earth, to the rivers, lakes and oceans, to the wind and the fires that rage—they are all me, and I am them. In this spaceship biosphere that we are living on, we all get recycled. We are reminded of this on Ash Wednesday, how very recyclable we are.

As I smudge my finger in the palm ashes and push back the hair from the brows of the Ash Wednesday participants who have come to take the sign of a cross, I say softly, "From dust you came and to dust you shall return" as I gently draw a cross on their foreheads with black soot. It's a sobering reminder that we are all connected through our very birth and death to one another, to creation, that all things capable of life are in fact, in one form or another, still living.

This comforts me.

Later, in a coffee shop, I overheard two older men talking about "little deaths." One of them was a wise old man—I could tell—who was giving advice to a younger man facing cancer. He talked about the "little deaths" in the form of all the things we lose, the car keys, the wallet, the life we once had, a loved one, our mobility, our freedom. He then said something about attunement.

I became aware that I was eavesdropping and stopped listening, though I could not help but smile. Attunement is simply the act of bringing all things into harmony. This wise old man was trying to help the other find harmony in the act of living and dying. It was a beautiful thing to experience, the exchange of loving and caring in the act of comforting through truthfulness and wisdom.

Each day, we have something to give to someone along the way—a smile, a word of encouragement, an expression of hope. Think of all the things the world gives us without ever asking for anything in return. The sun shines, as does the moon, creating day and night. We love the contrast of light and dark and the beautiful moments as the sun and moon change. The earth brings food, creation brings rain, and all the things that are needed for the conditions of life are provided for us for free. We have so much more to offer the earth and one another when we live each day in the mindfulness that we belong to an order much greater than ourselves. We have been invited to experience it, to become attuned to its natural rhythm, to rescue creation, each in our own small way, from the damages done.

To those of us who receive the mark of the cross and follow Christ on that journey of life and death and resurrection, this week and forever, let us meditate on that phrase "from ashes you came and to ashes you shall return." Let it be a reminder that though our bodies belong to the earth, our spirits were meant to soar, and we belong to a greater gift than we could ever give, made real to us every day in so many ways. The gift of life unending, the gift of the ashes.

14. The Alleluia Pulpit: Singing with Emmy Lou

No matter what I do, when I hear her voice, it is planted into some inner pocket of my soul that I cannot reach. I don't remember inviting her in. I suppose that's the way it is with spirits.

She is a silver-haired angel named Emmy Lou Harris, and she is a Nashville icon. She was singing in a church I had haunted once as an active participant, pre-divorce, during my rock band days, when I, too, was fabulous. The downtown church was Presbyterian, an Egyptian revivalist style sanctuary, that had survived since the late 1880s, and the atmosphere, for me, was rife with meaning.

It wasn't the first song she sang that touched me, but the second, a song of Alleluia against the odds—is there any other way to sing Alleluia?

Poetic and soul-justifying moments are like that, sung into the realities of everyday human existence, to those souls who are thirsty, empty, afraid, and alone, "as the deer pants for the water, so my heart longs after you . . . the Lord is my shepherd, I shall not want . . . though I walk through the valley of the shadow of death, I will fear no evil, for You are with me." Poetry like this is spoken against despair, the despair of the world that Emmy Lou expressed so piercingly.

While I was listening to Emmy Lou, I was reminded of another moment, my very first funeral as a pastor. I walked behind death itself, trailing the body in the silk-lined casket of an elderly lady I had never met. I wore a suit. It was October, the leaves were in full color, stiff and dying, but whispering in the wind against a cloudless corn blue sky. A lone bagpiper played hymns across the wide expanse of the well- populated graveyard. I was there as his protégé, to learn how to mediate death. An older pastor read in a beautiful cadence the twenty-third Psalm from his pocket-sized Book of Worship. Afterward, he quickly shook the hands of the grieving relatives and made his exit.

I followed, taking mental notes never to wear heels again to a funeral as I wrestled them from the soft grounds of the cemetery.

As I listened to Emmy Lou, I felt everything was being placed in perfect order, it was the same feeling I'd had at the graveyard. Everything was in order except for what I was feeling in my heart. How could she stand up there so composed and wield a power so fierce? How could I? How could ministers like myself dress in dark, well-tailored suits and offer up mediations for the dead? I don't know. I just know that it must be done, the order from the chaos.

Standing with a few hundred adoring fans of Emmy Lou, in this old, Egyptian revivalist church, I remembered that this was the one place I had felt at home in over a decade of wandering. It was a place where the faithful few gathered every Sunday, a place where we jointly cleaned up the urban alleyway beside the church from the repeated evidence of the social ills of the world, a place where we believed God inspired art could indeed usher in the reign of compassion and love into this broken world, inside a broken church. This had been a church to me, a church where I found a new life.

Off the corner of the stage, behind where Emmy Lou sang, there is a room full of photos and memorabilia that we affectionately named "the hall of the dead." It was lined with photos of pastors who had preached there Sunday after Sunday exactly where she stood, at the pulpit, and sang her Alleluia song. Pastors who agonized over building issues, the homeless and the sick, who wrote sermons at midnight on Saturday because they had spent the entire week on administrative tasks that they could not even remember and showed up at hospital beds at random hours during the week and presided over meetings, meals, funerals and weddings, and counseled those who had called at the last minute needing some immediate relief. Pastors who had also answered the endless doorbell ringing with the needs of the world (pastors whose dreams are haunted by door bells). Pastors who had tried their very best to save and resurrect this dying form of Christendom with their very souls because of the value it holds for others. She stood there where they had all stood, where I stand, too, in that hallowed but not so hallowed space, trying to make sense of the brokenness with whatever tools are at hand. It all seemed so much easier to produce magic when I, too, sang for the masses.

Even after preaching for a few years and searching for unique forms of crafting words, I find it hard to express the sense of awe and wonder one feels at the challenge of occupying this chasm, this verge, this pulpit of the world where we stand and try our best at singing.

After all, a thousand words cannot equal one perfectly honest Alleluia, sung in chorus with the gathered community. And no building or institution or even death can contain it. It sings without restraint, unbound by words, regardless of me.

A couple of years later, I shared the stage with Emmy Lou at another downtown church where I performed for a Christmas fundraiser for Nashville's homeless. I was thrilled to be performing on the same night as she and other musicians I admired. It took me back to a space I knew well, something I was good at, singing.

I met her back stage and we chatted.

I told her I was a preacher these days, to which she replied, filling her plate with finger sandwiches, "Well, I think singing is the highest form of prayer."

15. Peace Be Still: Giving Thanks as a Rebellious Act

Recently, I was out hiking with a friend I hadn't seen in years. We were in "his" mountains, the Appalachian range, of which there remained very few trails, valleys, or mountains he had not scaled, hiked, or skied. However, all of that changed as a series of life disasters—divorce, heart issues, and surgery— had stolen his zest and left him with a general apathy towards everything.

"So, how did you get better?" I asked. He came to a dead stop on the trail. First, he smiled, paused, and then said, "Giving thanks."

The irony was that "thanks be to God" had been his very own mantra that he had repeated to others throughout his life. And yet, in this crucial period of crisis, his mantra seemed to fail him. Perhaps the mantra had not quite fully penetrated his heart, as busy as he was, making his way in the world.

His intuitive therapist then put him on a daily regimen of "giving thanks."

Over time, my friend's mantra turned into a practice, and as it sank from his head to his heart, it became an act of rebellion against fear, doubt, and anxiety. He began his day giving thanks for everything, in defiance of his reality. He gave thanks for his life, his suffering, his relationships, his lack of relationships, the emptiness as well as the fullness, and the pain as well as the joy. He just began giving thanks all day long for everything, even for the disasters, and he gradually got better. Some of his physical issues remained, but gradually improved to a point he could tolerate, in other words, he could get out into his mountains again.

Gratitude as a practice changes your heart, and your heart changes you.

How does gratitude work? It's a mystery. But try it sometime, just for a day, and see how it alters your perspective. Observe how it makes you feel.

When I was growing up, we sang an old hymn, "Count your many blessings, name them one by one . . . count your many blessings see what God has done." I remember thinking about this on so many nights when I had trouble falling asleep. I would count my blessings, literally, and I was always surprised at the many positive things I could count, throughout the entirety of my life. I would always think of the kindness of people, provision when I thought there would be none, love in the oddest of places, and from all of that came peace, and from peace came rest.

Now, I try and practice gratitude throughout the day, particularly when things are rough. It becomes my daily act of rebellion against all the chaos that seems to rule the world. Gratitude may not change the landscape of the reality around me, but it does change my ability to deal with it, my ability to have internal peace.

Jesus spoke into the chaos, "Peace, peace be still." He spoke a presence, not just a phrase. It seems to me that Jesus, Divine presence in human form, knew this was an act of rebellion, stating something completely counteractive to the physical reality around him, and he practiced it constantly.

Poet and author, Deena Metzger, speaks about the importance of focusing on the sweetness in the nature of living things as a way toward spiritual renewal. She also says it's important not to cultivate gloom.[vi]

We focus as we practice speaking our gratitude defiantly into a world of chaos. As we do, the chaos, strangely, becomes more orderly or at the very least, manageable.

A few people have said to me that they find it impossible to focus on anything for longer than a minute or two, that their mind races forward and they feel they can't control it. Others tell me that they find it hard to focus on anything good when so much in the world is bad. I tenderly remind them that faith is a practice, it doesn't come instantaneously, and that much of our faith is about the focus on the goodness of God that penetrates doubt, fear and, anxiety. I encourage them that it is something we were intended to do, this ritual of spirit, and it is not that hard once you get going. In fact, it takes on a life of its own.

These realms of fear, anxiety, and doubt do exist, and the power in these realms is very real. We can spend our entire lives being driven by these forces, trying to numb them, outrun them, sometimes, even feeling crushed by them. However, there is a higher order that is capable of speaking peace and calm into this disordered realm where compulsions drive human behavior. We find this order in the rebellious act of being in a state of gratitude.

Giving thanks, the practice of gratitude, is a way through, a way to interrupt the cycle of anxiety and fear. It calms the chaos within and settles us into pursuits that bring real peace and joy, creating a channel within which the sacred has a stronger sway in our day-to-day world. Through this practice of giving thanks, we connect with the Great Spirit, God, who gives us peace, who sustains our hearts with joy and calmness and breath, we become more stabilized. Eventually, we begin to make better decisions about how we invest our time and energy, and we begin to trust our instincts as they are guided by the greater good.

Today, try a little rebellious exercise. Open your heart to the possibility of gratitude, open your heart to God, to newness, to thanks; and especially, in the midst of disaster. I know it's counter-intuitive to give thanks as a rebellious act, but what do you have to lose but fear itself? Give thanks, simply, for life in the midst. Go stare at a dogwood blossom for a few minutes, noticing every color of light springing forth. Count the times you discover a new freckle on your partner's face. Look deeply into a child's eyes. Get lost driving nowhere. Go stare at a river. Sit in silence with some relaxing music playing and recite the three-word mantra, until it becomes practice. Here is one.

Peace be still.

You can do it. Give yourself permission to try.

16. The Finding Your Voice Pose

A couple years into the pastorate, by pure and holy accident, I began doing yoga. A yoga studio had opened down the street and I stopped by to welcome them to the neighborhood. Melissa, who was about my age, an actress who still carried her SAG card, and her mom, Cindy, owned the studio. They talked me into my first hot yoga class by inviting me to walk around barefoot, something I could never resist anywhere.

The studio was pristine, with infrared heat for hot yoga, and new paint on the walls in the tones of day spa blue and sandstone. New floors that were just slightly abrasive and warm massaged my tired, bare feet, and I felt a sudden urge to grab a mat and lay down prostrate in complete surrender. Everything was new and deliciously appealing. What was even more appealing, I found as time went on, were the locked doors two minutes before class, no cell phone, no access—just me and the movement, the sweat, and the teacher's calming voice.

The healing, infrared heat would eventually pull out all the aches and the toxins I had accumulated and stored in my body from a sick church building. I found out later there had been, for a long time, very high CO_2 levels in my office due to a boiler leak and poor air circulation. CO_2 reduces the oxygen in the air, slowly taking your breath away as there is less available oxygen to breathe. What is ironic is that my job, which was to usher in a holy breath was literally taking my breath away. Each necessary system in my body—nervous, cardiovascular, muscular—had begun to feel sluggish, basically anything that needed good oxygen. On top of that, the ongoing stresses and strains of the emotional roller coaster of a church on the verge of dying or coming to life depending on the week had me in a constant state of whiplash. I needed yoga, even though I hadn't realized it at the time.

Melissa told me that yoga would change my life. I realized later that it not only changed my life, but it saved my body. I still do hot yoga and I am still recovering my breath, little by little, which, coincidentally, is synonymous with overcoming fear.

There is a pose in my yoga class called "standing separate leg, head to knee." The main design of this pose enables you to safely encounter claustrophobia and help you find your voice. It's interesting that claustrophobia and the inner voice are linked, and overcoming the one leads to the discovery of the other.

To do this pose, you tuck your chin into your chest, place one foot about three feet in front of the other and bend down with your hands above your head in prayer. As your hands touch the floor, you bend your head to touch your knee and breathe only twenty percent of your normal intake of air. You are effectively trapping yourself on purpose so that your oxygen is deliberately reduced. You hold this pose for thirty seconds then do it again facing the opposite direction.

In this yoga pose, you are deliberately cutting off your breath for a few moments to overcome your fear and find your voice. You are placing a tourniquet on the general oxygen flow so that you might focus on something very specific, the fear of not having an escape.

Most people think claustrophobia is the fear of small, enclosed spaces. However, this sudden onset of sheer panic can appear in places that are wide open, too, like driving down the interstate or hiking in the woods. It is the fear of not having an exit, the fear of not being able to find the way out from a situation or experience that you perceive is trapping you.

Placing yourself in this "standing separate leg, head to knee" position mimics that claustrophobic fear so that you can discover a method of breathing your way through it. This is how you slowly and gradually find your voice, through this gentle practice of sending your breath to the problem at hand.

A voice can be barely audible, like a breath. Of course, we have our unique and God-given voices with our unique tones. When we speak and sing, the ones who know us can easily recognize our voice and identify us by our individual tone. However, when we speak of "finding our voice," we are often referring to something different than the intricate ballet that occurs in our vocal chords to create our unique, audible sound. The "voice" of this yoga pose and our spiritual life quest generally refers to something subtle. It is that essence of you that resonates with the essence of God, much like a tuning fork that reaches and sustains its pure tone once the overtones have died out.

The key to finding this voice is learning to distinguish between the overtones and the pure tone that embodies your voice. The twenty percent breathing that the yoga posture temporarily induces helps eliminate the excess so that you are forced to discover what is genuine, and enables you to feel the difference between overtones and pure tones in your very being. Sometimes it's necessary to subtract rather than add to our situations in life to hear the inner voice, that pure tone.

    I suppose the most difficult aspect of discovering the pure tone is that it does not advertise or try to compete with other, more dissonant overtones. While overtones distract and distort the pure tone, if you wait long enough, they eventually die out, and you discover the one note that you are trying to hear; however, this requires patience and a certain curiosity of what it is you are searching for. Ultimately, you will find it because it is there waiting to be discovered, often beneath a great deal of excessive noise.

    The question then becomes, when you begin to resonate with the pure tone that is the breath of God in you, how will you be then? What will be different? How will you know that you are different?

    I can speak from my own very delayed arrival at the foothills of the voice. It is not quite like Kilimanjaro or anything as obvious and monolithic. It is more like a continuum that I have been searching for my whole life; a tone that I am attuning myself to. More and more, I feel that I'm inclined to put my precious energy into what I love. What I love has deep and abiding worth, not in monetary terms but in life terms, such as relationships; the gifts that I have developed over time; spending time in nature; engaging less in hollow entertainment; eating better foods; consuming less bad foods; worrying less, meditating more; finally letting go of the resentments I have stored up due to past hurt. This is my daily mantra—letting the light in and finding my voice.

It also means hiding less and learning to be myself, not some projection of what I feel I am supposed to be. The hardest part is that if I am to attune myself to the pure tone of the inner voice that is my True Self, I must "tune out" other tones. And this is a greater discipline than I ever imagined.

It is not really asking, after all, "What is God?" but rather, "What is not God?" God is there at the central being of us all, the pure tone; waiting to be discovered.

17. Woman Gone Fishing, Be Back...Maybe

When I left for college, I left fishing too, and that's when a part of my soul went missing.

When I was a young girl, I didn't think much about fishing, it's just what we did to catch fish. We dug up earthworms, threaded them carefully so that the writhing tail swished in the water, covering the sharp hook, and waited with excitement for the bobber to go under. I even baited my own hook, a question many people seem to ask me when I say I've taken up fishing again. I caught my first large-mouth bass at age six at Ms. Loduska's pond, a secret, swampy fishing hole hidden down a country road.

A lifetime later, I felt the urge to fish again because I have been away far too long. Fishing is an act of soul conjuring. I am not the first to make the connection between fishing and the soul. Jesus used the metaphor of fishing often to speak of luring the soul from the depths, no longer fisher*men* but fishers *of* men.

Perhaps Jesus had a different metaphor for the women, or perhaps the women who stayed by his side didn't require a metaphor for bringing souls into the world from the depths, some things are just second nature. Perhaps they baited their own hooks too.

At the Tennessee Wildlife Refuge lake where I decided to take up fishing again the brown and yellow sign read "Fishermen Must Register." I assumed the sign meant that even though I'm a woman, I still had to register my intention to pull fish from the water. Like most women, I find that there are many "man-made" barriers in this world, and I've just learned to overlook them to do what I need to do. It's a trick I learned from fishing: you go where the fish are calling—through fences, briars, sometimes out into the deep, deep water, out beyond signs warning that you do not belong. You learn to listen to what is under the surface and cast your line there. It's just how you catch fish.

Like Mary Magdalene, breaking all the rules to find her true self, sensing some route to her very own soul was there at Jesus' feet. She was not going to let a few men prevent her from throwing herself down and spending everything precious she owned to know the truth, even though she probably knew full well that she would be shamed for it, it was her nature to do so, to go where her soul was calling. Nature is always breaking the rules we set for ourselves to show us the beauty of our souls.

There is something that calls to us from beneath the surface of the seen world, something that lives just below what we know through conscious reasoning. The soul has a way of calling us out beyond our own logical conclusions, on a day when we should be getting some work done, the perfect blue-sky calls out to our imagination to simply come fishing. To cast a lure out to gently pierce the tranquil lid of the seen world for something that is wanting to come to the surface of our lives. The soul has a way of revealing itself as we follow our sometimes impractical instincts, if only we will take a moment to listen and respond. Sometimes we are fishing for fish and sometimes we are fishing just to get a little glimpse of our soul. Sometimes these acts are one in the same.

This act of fishing was more than a re-enactment of childhood memories, it was another way of loving the beauty hidden inside of me and inviting it to come to the surface of my life. Maybe I would even catch a fish or two.

There were two retired African American men fishing just down the trail from me, and having a great time. They looked to be in their seventies, which meant they had lived through much harder times than I could imagine, more discrimination and shaming than I had felt in a lifetime, most likely. Still, they had mercy on a white woman, giving me three juicy earthworms because my $3.59 lure wasn't doing the trick.

I thanked them and headed past their spot into a more remote part of the bank. I was looking for some solitude and shade.

"It's nice back there," they said, "but watch out for papa goose around the corner. He's sitting on a batch of eggs and he's likely to attack."

Forewarned, I spoke to father goose about passing and, begrudgingly, he showed his long pink tongue and hissed while mother goose swam off the shore, a few feet away to run interference.

As soon as I got past the geese, it was as if I had cast my line into a hidden world. All sorts of alarms began going off—large American toads bellowed, signaling my arrival, their trills echoing off the hills across the lake, announcing my invasion into Eden. Two more geese landed on the water and began doing a formal ritual I've never seen before, swimming toward one another and turning, in the exact same rhythm, and swimming apart in a straight line as if they were pacing off for a duel. A blue heron flew low, an opportunist, skimming the water for a quick snack, and a small, brown snake swam beneath my bare feet that were dangling in the shallow water off the fishing dock.

    I had penetrated the territory of the unseen and found it to be incredibly serene, even with all the noise. Whenever I venture into nature, I always find I am entering both Eden and my deepest self.

    As I cast my rod and reel in a cadence—click, cast, plop, and then the long, slow winding of the slightly taut line, I thought a great deal about mother earth, about what is hidden beneath the surface, calling, in subtle tones, to be revealed. I thought of the many things women are taught to hide about themselves, to be ashamed of. I thought of all the fishing we must do in ourselves to find those things, to bring them to the surface, all the barriers we must break down, the intuition we must learn to follow, the briar patches within we wade through, the no trespassing signs we must ignore.

    I thought of the very cycle of womanhood itself, the vulnerability of the emotions in the rising and falling of various chemicals and fluids that are produced each month in a woman's body in a seemingly inconvenient and strange ballet of order. The ways in which the difference of being feminine causes so much disorder in the world because it does not fit into the structure of being regularly productive, emotionally together, neat, and tidy, it does not even fit on the official wildlife refuge "fishermen must register" sign

As I sat on the banks of a lake and cast a line into the deep water, I realized mother nature has a way of revealing what is hidden, for those who would take the time to listen. She has a way of ordering what is wild without sacrificing one ounce of wildness, of bringing calmness into chaos without apologizing for her disasters, of finding what has gone missing if you are willing to break through a few barriers for the search. I realized a woman's true nature is close to the heart of creation, whatever she does in the world, she brings this creative energy to play just by living close to her heart.

At a time in our world when the statistics tell us that one out of every three women worldwide is a victim of violence, it is vital that women (and men) go fishing for creative energy within themselves—that which heals, orders, and renews, giving life to brokenness. It is time to claim a woman's body for something more than violence. There, in the depths, beyond the barriers, just beneath the surface, a woman's soul awaits herself, if only she will choose to go fishing.

18. Growing Hollow

Sanity and order still exist in this world in a realm known as nature. I am not a nature worshipper, but a nature lover. I fall more deeply in love with the natural world the longer I spend on this earth. It is roaming through nature in its truest form that I will miss when I leave this world, both in the wild and the tame, and inside every person I meet who allows me to see a little piece of their soul.

There is a force in the world that moves through everything, the ancients had a word for it, *ruach* in Hebrew; it means the breath or wind or spirit of God. If you listen to your own breath or listen to any screech, bellow, echo, or song of any wild thing, you hear a music that is creation blowing through the hollow of living things. How can you not? When we listen to our breath, to the wind in the trees, to the quiet of our breathing in and out, we experience a sense of our truer nature. We connect with *ruach* and we feel a sense of home.

Of course, we don't understand it fully, we have tried desperately to replace it with another force, that forcefulness of progress at any cost. We have ended up with vast realms of conquered wilderness, erased rain forests and polluted sanctuaries. We have not only done this to our world, we have also done it to the realm of our souls; for our souls are the very wilderness spaces within us, the place where God roams freely and wild, connecting us to the nature of the eternal. We have treated wilderness spaces, nature and soul alike, as barriers rather than partners in progress. Now we rely on what little wildlife sanctuary is left in our world to somehow renew itself and give us hope again. The hope of our being is uniquely linked to the thriving of our natural world. We can no longer afford to demand that mother nature submit to the domination of progress. What's more, she seems to be done as well.

It doesn't matter whether you believe in climate change or not, it is upon us. Now the scientific community seems to agree that if we fail to figure out how to live in harmony, catastrophic consequences will occur, and some will occur anyway, regardless of how much we can reduce our CO_2 emissions. Still it's clear. We must act to soothe the imbalance of nature.

Though it may seem hopeless, I take my inspiration from the Redwood trees. Not one tree has been as depleted by deforestation as deeply as the Redwood. Of the earth's oldest trees only five percent of Redwoods remain. Still, if they are given the opportunity, they will renew over time, slowly, methodically, and faithfully as a community of the ancient and the new.

I recently visited a few Redwood forest groves where young Redwoods are thriving beside ancient giants. We could learn a great deal about how we adapt to change from these magnificent trees and how to find a measure of order out of chaos.

How do they do it? These trees create clonal colonies around a mother tree. The mother tree can be completely burned out and hollow on the inside while other clone trees take on the growth around her, creating a circle of trees that many nature lovers refer to as a fairy ring. Not only do these trees continue the growth the mother tree began, but they form a circle of protection around her as she continues her growth. The Redwoods don't need their insides to live, they continue to grow hollow, perhaps because they are surrounded by such a devoted community they can risk becoming empty.

We are all members of the earth, made from dust and breath and the evolving of life itself. As I say every Ash Wednesday when I make the sign of the cross on foreheads with palm ash, "From dust you came and to dust you shall return"; a reminder of our temporal status in the whole scheme of things.

Perhaps it is time for us to circle up, remember where we came from. Earth work is soul work is spirit work. Perhaps it is time for us to circle nature and those hollow spaces inside of us that long for home and help it all grow. The time is always now to explore more deeply how our human and soul nature is connected to the nature of creation itself.

The poet Hafiz said, "Make your ribcage hollow like a flute so God can play music in you." Often, making a real connection with what gives us life, the Divine breath of God, means that we have to risk growing hollow. Just like the redwoods, we need a community to circle up around us so that we can risk growing into our natural selves. I have often thought that the church is such a place, a community that can hold you, circle up around you, while you take the risk of emptying yourself of all your grief, pain, resentment, and fear. A sacred grove in the civilized world. We all need a community to hold us while we risk growing hollow enough to hear the music of God.

There seems to be a great measure of sanity awaiting us as we give ourselves over to this Divine force in the world, this hollow *ruach* that moves and lives in everything, this breath of God.

About the Author:

Sherry Cothran, M.Div., is a speaker, musician, author and ordained minister. In addition to her ongoing work as senior pastor, Sherry has been featured in USA Today, UMC.org, led at Festival of Homiletics, was the Artist in Residence, 2015, at Louisville Presbyterian Seminary and the recipient of two grants from the Louisville Institute. Her sermons and blogs have been featured in *Good Preacher, Abingdon Women, The Interpreter, Ministry Matters, Alive Now*. An award winning recording artist, her most recent collaboration with indie film maker, Tracy Facceli, "Tending Angels" can be viewed on You Tube. Sherry is regularly booked as a keynote speaker, workshop leader and performer of songs and stories. For more information, go to www.sherrycothran.com

*Photo by Alison Harpole

Notes

[i] Jalaluddin Mevlana Rumi, 13th Century Sufi Poet, translation unknown.

[ii] Jean Vanier, *From Brokeness to Community*, (Mahwah: Paulist Press, 1992).

[iii] Hafiz, 14th Century Sufi Poet, translation unknown.

[iv] Steven Spielberg, 2016, May 21, "Steven Spielberg Listens to the Whispers of His Intuition" Goalcast: https://www.youtube.com/watch?v=l2Im25BdQ8M

[v] Frederick Beuchner, *Wishful Thinking: A Seeker's ABC*, (San Francisco: Harper One, 1993).

[vi] Deena Metzger, *Entering the Ghost River*, (Hand to Hand, 2002).